USING THIS BOOK

*One of the best ways of helping children to learn to read is by reading stories to them and with them. This way they learn what **reading** is, and they will gradually come to recognise many words, and begin to read for themselves.*

First, grown-ups read the story on the left-hand pages aloud to the child.

You can reread the story as often as the child enjoys hearing it. Talk about the pictures as you go.

Later the child is encouraged to read the words under the pictures on the right-hand page.

Further suggestions for helping your child to read are given in the Parent/Teacher booklet.

British Library Cataloguing in Publication Data
McCullagh, Sheila K.
   How Miranda flew down Puddle Lane.
   —(Puddle Lane reading programme. Stage 1; v. 16)
   I. Title   II. Dillow, John   III. Series
   823'.914[J]   PZ7
   ISBN 0-7214-0922-9

First edition

Published by Ladybird Books Ltd Loughborough Leicestershire UK
Ladybird Books Inc Lewiston Maine 04240 USA

Printed in England

How Miranda flew down Puddle Lane

written by SHEILA McCULLAGH
illustrated by JOHN DILLOW

This book belongs to:

Ladybird Books

*If you haven't read any books about the
Wideawake Mice read this aloud first.*

The Wideawake Mice were once toy mice,
in Mr Wideawake's shop, in Candletown.
But one day a magician accidentally
spilt magic silver dust all over them,
and they came alive.

They escaped from the toy shop, and
went to live in the market building,
in the middle of the square.

This is a story about Miranda Mouse,
and what happened when she went for a
walk in Puddle Lane.

Miranda Mouse

One afternoon, the Wideawake Mice
were all fast asleep, in their home
in Candletown Market.
The sun was shining down outside,
and the mice were all very warm
and comfortable.

A bee came buzzing in under the roof.
The bee buzzed in Miranda's ear.
Miranda woke up.
The bee flew off, into the sunshine.

Miranda woke up.

Miranda looked down at the stones below.
She could see the sunlight,
shining on the stones.
There was no one in the building.
Miranda blew in her brother's ear.
Jeremy Mouse opened one eye.
"I'm going out," she said.
"Come with me, Jeremy."
But Jeremy was much too sleepy
to get up. He shut his eye,
and went back to sleep.

''I'm going out,''
said Miranda.
Jeremy opened
one eye.

Miranda looked at the other mice.
They were all fast asleep.
"**I'm** going out," said Miranda.
Nobody else said anything at all.
They didn't even twitch their tails.

"I'm going out,"
said Miranda.

Miranda ran to the top of a post.
She took off her clothes, and
folded them very carefully.
Then she ran down the post
to the ground below.

Miranda ran down
the post.

Tom Cat was sitting on a wall
in the sunshine.
He was fast asleep.
As Miranda ran out into the square,
Tom Cat opened one eye.
Miranda didn't see Tom Cat.
She ran off, across the square.

Tom Cat opened
one eye.
Miranda didn't see
Tom Cat.

Miranda ran along the street.
Tom Cat got up.
He jumped down from the wall.

Tom Cat
jumped down.

Miranda looked up Puddle Lane.
She didn't see anyone.
(Miranda wasn't very big,
and she was looking for people
the same size as her.)

Miranda looked up
Puddle Lane.

Miranda ran up Puddle Lane.
She hadn't gone far,
when she heard a crash!

Miranda ran up
Puddle Lane.

Miranda hid.

She hid in an empty box.

She kept quite still.

She listened.

Nothing happened.

Miranda looked out of the box.

She didn't see anyone.

Miranda hid.

Miranda ran on, up Puddle Lane.
She hadn't gone far,
when she heard a clatter!

Miranda ran up
Puddle Lane.

Miranda hid.

(She felt rather frightened.)

She hid in a dark corner.

She kept quite still, and
she listened.

Nothing happened.

Miranda looked out of the corner.

She didn't see anyone.

Miranda hid.

Miranda ran on, up Puddle Lane.
She hadn't gone far,
when she heard a thud!

Miranda ran up
Puddle Lane.

Miranda hid.

She hid in an empty jar.

She kept quite still.

She listened.

Nothing happened.

Miranda looked out of the jar.

She didn't see anyone.

Miranda hid.

Miranda ran on, up Puddle Lane.
She had gone a long way,
when she came to a big foot.

Miranda ran up
Puddle Lane.

The big foot was in a big shoe.
The Magician lived at one end
of Puddle Lane, and the foot
was the Magician's foot.
Miranda didn't know what it was.
She climbed up on to the Magician's shoe.

Miranda and the big foot

The Magician looked down.
He saw Miranda.
Miranda was just going to climb
up the Magician's leg,
when she heard a deep voice say,
"What are you doing in Puddle Lane?
It's not very safe for you here,
little mouse.
You'd better go home again."

The Magician
looked down.
He saw Miranda.

"Fly through the air, little mouse!"
cried the Magician.
"Fly through the air —
and you're back in the square!"

The Magician snapped his fingers.

Miranda found herself flying
through the air.
She flew down Puddle Lane,
round the corner, and back
into Market Square.

Miranda flew down
Puddle Lane.

She landed by the post
in Candletown Market.
"Whatever happened?" cried Miranda.
"Whatever happened to me?
I think I had better go home.
I'll go back to Jeremy,
and tell him all about it."
And she did.

And that is the end
of this story.

Miranda went back
to Jeremy.

When Miranda looked up Puddle Lane,
she couldn't see anyone.
How many people can **you** see in
Puddle Lane?